THE AMERICAN FLAG

A TRUE BOOK

by
Patricia Ryon Quiri

Children's Press®
A Division of Grolier Publishing
New York London Hong Kong Sydney
Danbury, Connecticut

Reading Consultant
Linda Cornwell
Learning Resource Consultant
Indiana Department
of Education

Author's Dedication:
For my son Brad, who has
given me fifteen years of joy.
Love,
Mom

An American flag in front of
the Washington Monument

Visit Children's Press on the Internet at:
http://publishing.grolier.com

Library of Congress Cataloging-in-Publication Data

Quiri, Patricia Ryon.
    The American flag / by Patricia Ryon Quiri.
        p.   cm. — (A true book)
    Includes bibliographical references and index.
    Summary: Describes the history and symbolism of the American flag.
    ISBN 0-516-20617-6 (lib.bdg.)   0-516-26370-6 (pbk.)
    1. Flags—United States—Juvenile literature. [1. Flags—United States.]
I. Title. II. Series.
CR113.Q57 1998
929.9'2'0973—dc21   97-517
                                                                     CIP
                                                                     AC

Contents

A Symbol of Freedom

The American flag is a symbol of freedom. It stands for the land, the people, and the government of the United States. Nicknames for the American flag are Old Glory, the Stars and Stripes, and the Star-Spangled Banner. The people of the United States are proud of their flag and the country for which it stands.

Flags and Their History

Long ago, before flags were made of cloth, people made flaglike symbols out of different materials. Wood, stone, metal, and even animal skins were used. These symbols were called standards. They were placed on top of spears or poles and carried into battle.

6

Ancient Roman soldiers carrying standards (above) and the flag of Denmark (right)

They were also used as symbols of land ownership.

Historians, people who study the past, believe that the first flag to stand for a country was the flag of Denmark—a white cross on a red background.

In 1219, Denmark's King Valdemar saw a white cross in the red sky just before he won a battle.

Also in the 1200s, England used a flag called St. George's Cross. It had a simple design— a red cross on a white background. Scotland, a country to the north of England, had a flag called St. Andrew's Cross. That cross was white, but it was shaped like an X. The background of the flag was blue.

St. George's Cross (left), St. Andrew's Cross, (middle), and the Union Jack (right)

In 1606, these two flags merged, or joined, because England and Scotland had united under King James I in 1603. The new flag was called the Union Jack. It became the first official flag of Great Britain. In the early days, Great Britain ruled the American colonies.

9

Early American Flags

The colony of Virginia was founded in North America in 1607 by English settlers. They claimed the land for Great Britain and flew the Union Jack. In time, more colonies were settled along the Atlantic coast. Soon there were thirteen, all ruled by Great Britain. The Union Jack flew over these colonies for about 150 years.

During the 1700s, the colonies grew angry with Great Britain. The British government wanted too much control over them. It taxed the colonists on many goods, such as sugar and tea. The colonists wanted freedom from British rule. They wanted to make their own laws.

The Revolutionary War began in 1775. It was fought between Great Britain and the thirteen colonies. In 1776, the colonists declared their independence from Britain.

In the early days of the war, many different flags were made in the colonies. Some

Two of the many flags flown by American colonists during the Revolutionary War

DONT TREAD ON ME

colonists used pine trees on their banners as a symbol of hardiness, or strength. Others sewed rattlesnakes on their flags with the words "Don't Tread On Me."

In 1775, at Benjamin Franklin's suggestion, the American colonies designed a flag of their own. In the upper left-hand corner was a little Union Jack. The rest of the flag was made up of thirteen horizontal stripes. Seven were red and six were white. These stripes stood for the thirteen colonies. That flag was called the Grand Union flag. It was also known as the Cambridge flag and the Continental flag.

Many American ships flew the Grand Union flag during the Revolutionary War.

It was never an official United States flag, but up until July 4, 1776, many American ships flew the Grand Union. Then, on June 14, 1777, Congress passed the first law about the American flag.

A New Flag

The new law stated that the flag would have thirteen red and white stripes and thirteen white stars on a blue background. The stripes and stars stood for the thirteen colonies.

There were no rules about how many points the stars should have or how the stars

For the first official U.S. flag, there were no rules about how the thirteen stars should be placed.

should be placed. Some flags were made with five-pointed stars and others were made with six-pointed stars. On some flags, the stars were set in rows while on others, they were set in circles. Some flags had seven red stripes, some had six.

The red, white, and blue colors of the flag were symbols, too. Red stood for courage. White stood for purity or goodness. Blue stood for justice.

Who made the first flag with Stars and Stripes? No one knows for sure. The best-known tale is the one about Betsy Ross. According to the story, George Washington and two other men went to the home of Betsy Ross in Philadelphia in June 1776. They asked her to make a new flag for the United States. She looked at their sketches and changed only one thing. She changed the number of points on the stars from six to five.

The Betsy ★ ★
★ ★ Ross Myth

The well-known story about Betsy Ross meeting with George Washington to make the first official flag is very popular among schoolchildren. Although Betsy Ross was a flagmaker, most historians doubt the truth of this story.

Most historians do not believe Betsy Ross made the first Stars and Stripes. Records do show, however, that Betsy was paid for making a flag for the Pennsylvania navy in May 1777.

Another person who claimed he made the first Stars and Stripes was a New Jersey man named Francis Hopkinson. He had signed the Declaration of Independence. Hopkinson sent a letter to

Francis Hopkinson

Congress asking to be paid for his flag design. But Congress did not pay him. They felt that many other people had helped design the new flag.

We will probably never know who created the first official

flag of the United States. The important thing is that Americans honor their flag. One special day to do this is on Flag Day, celebrated every year on June 14.

American children celebrating Flag Day

Changes in the Flag

The United States of America grew quickly. By 1794, Vermont and Kentucky had also joined the Union. These states wanted to be represented on the flag too. So, in 1795, a flag was made with fifteen stars and fifteen stripes. This second official flag of the United States was used from

Francis Scott Key (right) and the actual "Star-Spangled Banner" (left) he wrote about in his famous poem

1795 until 1818. This "Star-Spangled Banner" was the flag that Francis Scott Key wrote a famous poem about. In time, that poem became the country's national anthem.

Key wrote his famous poem during the War of 1812, when the United States was once again at war with Britain. In September 1814, Key, an American lawyer and poet, watched a battle at Fort McHenry in Baltimore from a nearby ship. "By the dawn's early light," he was thrilled to see "that the flag was still there." He found a piece of paper in his pocket and wrote the words that described his

Francis Scott Key watching the battle at Fort McHenry that inspired his poem

joy. Later, his words were set to an old English tune. On March 3, 1931, President Herbert Hoover made the "Star-Spangled Banner" the national anthem of the United States.

A Growing Nation

After 1818, more and more states joined the Union. But if a new stripe were added for each new state, the flag would get too big. Congressman Peter H. Wendover of New York City had an idea. He suggested that the number of stripes should always be thirteen in honor of

Over the years, as more states joined the Union, more stars were added to the flag.

the thirteen original states, and that a star should be added for each new state that joined the Union.

Congress passed the third Flag Act of the United States on April 4, 1818. It agreed that whenever a state was added, a new flag would fly on the next Fourth of July. This is still the law today.

By 1912, the Union had forty-eight states. President William Howard Taft decided

The forty-eight-star flag was the official flag from 1912 to 1959.

that the people needed rules about how big the flag could be and where the stars should be placed. A new flag was designed with six rows of eight stars. This flag lasted from 1912 to 1959 and represented the United States in World Wars I and II.

The last two states admitted to the Union were Alaska (on January 3, 1959) and Hawaii (on August 21, 1959). These two states brought the total number of stars on the flag to fifty. The fifty-star flag is the twenty-

The current, fifty-star flag was unveiled by President Eisenhower after Hawaii joined the Union in 1959.

seventh official flag of the United States since the first Flag Law of 1777.

The Pledge of Allegiance

In the late 1800s, American schoolchildren raised money to buy flags for their schools. A pledge to the flag was written and published in 1892 by Francis Bellamy and James B. Upham.

The original pledge was a little different from the one

The PLEDGE to the FLAG

I PLEDGE ALLEGIANCE
to the FLAG of the
UNITED STATES of AMERICA
and to the REPUBLIC for which
IT STANDS
ONE NATION INDIVISIBLE
with LIBERTY and JUSTICE
for ALL

The version of the Pledge of Allegiance that was used before 1954

Schoolchildren reciting the Pledge of Allegiance

children know today. It pledged allegiance to "my flag." This was not clear enough because it might sound as if immigrants were pledging allegiance to their old country. In 1923, the words were changed to "the flag of the United States of America." The words "under God" were added on June 14, 1954. When people recite the Pledge of Allegiance, they are promising to be loyal to the United States of America.

Honoring the American Flag

Many rules have been made about how the American flag should be treated. For example, the flag should be raised up the flagpole quickly and lowered slowly. It should not be flown in bad weather unless it is an all-weather (waterproof) flag.

The flag should be raised up the flag-pole quickly and lowered slowly.

The flag should be flown from sunrise until sunset. It may be flown at night only if it is properly lit. And the flag should never touch the ground.

When the flag passes by, Americans are supposed to put their right hands over their hearts.

When the flag passes, as in a parade, or when one recites the Pledge of Allegiance, one should face the flag and place one's right hand over one's heart.

Also, many rules have been made about flying the flag at half-mast—halfway up the flagpole. The flag is flown at half-mast to honor someone

Flags at half-mast

who has died. It is flown at half-mast on Memorial Day to honor those Americans who died fighting for their country. It is also flown at half-mast when a president or other government official dies.

The American flag stands for the people and ideals of the United States. It should always be treated with respect.

There is a proper way to
fold the American flag
when putting it away.

To Find Out More

Here are some additional resources to help you learn more about the American flag:

 **Books**

Haban, Rita. **How Proudly They Wave: Flags of the Fifty States.** Lerner Publications, 1989.

Kent, Deborah. **The Star-Spangled Banner.** Children's Press, 1995.

Munoz Ryan, Pam. **The Flag We Love.** Charlesbridge Publishing, 1996.

Quiri, Patricia Ryon. **The National Anthem.** Children's Press, 1998.

White, David. **The Great Book of Flags.** Rourke Enterprises, 1989.

Organizations and Online Sites

Betsy Ross House
239 Arch Street
Philadelphia, PA 19106
*http://libertynet.org/iha/
betsy/index.html*

Tour the Betsy Ross House, find out how to make a five-pointed star "in one snip," and learn the history of the American flag, as well as plenty of flag trivia.

Flag Education and Etiquette
http://www.legion.org/flag-toc.htm

This site, provided by the American Legion, tells all about flag practices and etiquette.

Flags
http://www.law.uoknow.edu/flags.html

See the various flags from U.S. history, as well as the official flags of all fifty states, territories, and possessions.

Flag of the United States of America
http://www.geocities.com/CapitolHill/4182/

History and timeline of the American flag with dozens of links to related sites, including state home pages.

National Flag Foundation
Flag Plaza
Pittsburgh, PA 15219-3630
800-615-1776
http://www.icss.com/usflag/nff.html

The National Flag Foundation provides lots of information about flags and their history.

Pledge of Allegiance
http://www.vineyard.net/vineyard/history/pledge.htm

Learn all about Francis Bellamy and the pledge he wrote.

Important Words

allegiance devotion, loyalty

anthem song of praise

colony region of land ruled by a foreign country

independence freedom

justice fair treatment for all

merge join together

official recognized, formal

pledge promise

protesting expressing one's opinion against something

resolution the act of coming to a decision

standard flaglike symbol on a spear or pole

symbol something that stands for another thing

Index

Meet the Author

Patricia Ryon Quiri lives in Palm Harbor, Florida, with her husband, Bob, and three sons. Ms. Quiri graduated from Alfred University in upstate New York with a B.A. in education. She is currently an elementary schoolteacher in the Pinellas County school district. Other Children's Press books by Ms. Quiri include *The Bald Eagle*, *Ellis Island*, *The National Anthem*, and *The Statue of Liberty*, as well as a six-book series on American government.